Managing Editor
Ina Massler Levin, M.A.

Editor-in-Chief
Sharon Coan, M.S. Ed.

Illustrators
Blanca Apodaca
Theresa M. Wright

Cover Artist
Barb Lorseyedi

Art Coordinator
Kevin Barnes

Art Direrctor
CJae Froshay

Product Manager
Phil Garcia

Publisher
Mary D. Smith, M.S. Ed.

Alphabet

Practice Makes Perfect

Authors

Sylvia Stone and Holly Bye

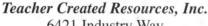

Teacher Created Resources, Inc.
6421 Industry Way
Westminster, CA 92683
www.teachercreated.com

ISBN: 978-0-7439-3328-5

©2002 Teacher Created Resources, Inc.
Reprinted, 2008
Made in U.S.A.

Table of Contents

Introduction 3
The Alphabet—Uppercase Flashcards 4
The Alphabet—Lowercase Flashcards 6
Alphabet Stories A and B 8
    Letter Aa 9
    Letter Bb 10
Alphabet Stories C and D 11
    Letter Cc 12
    Letter Dd 13
Alphabet Stories E and F 14
    Letter Ee 15
    Letter Ff 16
Alphabet Stories G and H 17
    Letter Gg 18
    Letter Hh 19
Alphabet Stories I and J 20
    Letter Ii 21
    Letter Jj 22
Alphabet Stories K and L 23
    Letter Kk 24
    Letter Ll 25
Alphabet Stories M and N 26
    Letter Mn 27
    Letter Nn 28
Alphabet Stories O and P 29
    Letter Oo 30
    Letter Pp 31
Alphabet Stories Q and R 32
    Letter Qq 33
    Letter Rr 34
Alphabet Stories S and T 35
    Letter Ss 36
    Letter Tt 37
Alphabet Stories U and V 38
    Letter Uu 38
    Letter Vv 40
Alphabet Stories W and X 41
    Letter Ww 42
    Letter Xx 43
Alphabet Stories Y and Z 44
    Letter Yy 45
    Letter Zz 46
Do You Know Your Alphabet? 47
Which Letters Are Missing? 48

Introduction

The old adage "practice makes perfect" can really hold true for your child and his or her education. The more practice and exposure your child has with concepts being taught in school, the more success he or she is likely to find. For many parents, knowing how to help their children may be frustrating because the resources may not be readily available.

As a parent it is also difficult to know where to focus your efforts so that the extra practice your child receives at home supports what he or she is learning in school.

This book has been written to help parents and teachers reinforce basic skills with children. *Practice Makes Perfect: Alphabet* introduces the alphabet. The exercises in this book can be done sequentially or can be taken out of order, as needed.

The following standards or objectives will be met or reinforced by completing the practice pages included in this book. These standards and objectives are similar to the ones required by your state and school district.

- The student will demonstrate competence in recognizing letters.
- The student will demonstrate competence in recognizing letter names.
- The student will demonstrate competence in forming uppercase letters.
- The student will demonstrate competence in forming lowercase letters.
- The student will demonstrate beginning phonemic awareness. (Phonemic awareness is the knowledge that every word consists of a sequence of sounds.)

How to Make the Most of This Book

Here are some useful ideas for making the most of this book:

- Set aside a specific place in your home to work on this book. Keep it neat and tidy, with the necessary materials on hand.

- Set up a certain time of day to work on these practice pages to establish consistency, or look for times in your day or week that are less hectic and more conducive to practicing skills.

- Keep all practice sessions with your child positive and constructive. If your child becomes frustrated or tense, set the book aside and look for another time to practice. Forcing your child to perform will not help. Do not use this book as a punishment.

- Help beginning readers with instructions.

- Review the work your child has done.

- Allow the child to use whatever writing instruments he or she prefers. For example, colored pencils can add variety and pleasure to drill work.

- Pay attention to the areas in which your child has the most difficulty. Provide extra guidance and exercises in those areas.

- Look for ways to make real-life application to the skills being reinforced. Play games with your child by looking for words that use the letters he or she is practicing.

The Alphabet—Uppercase Flashcards

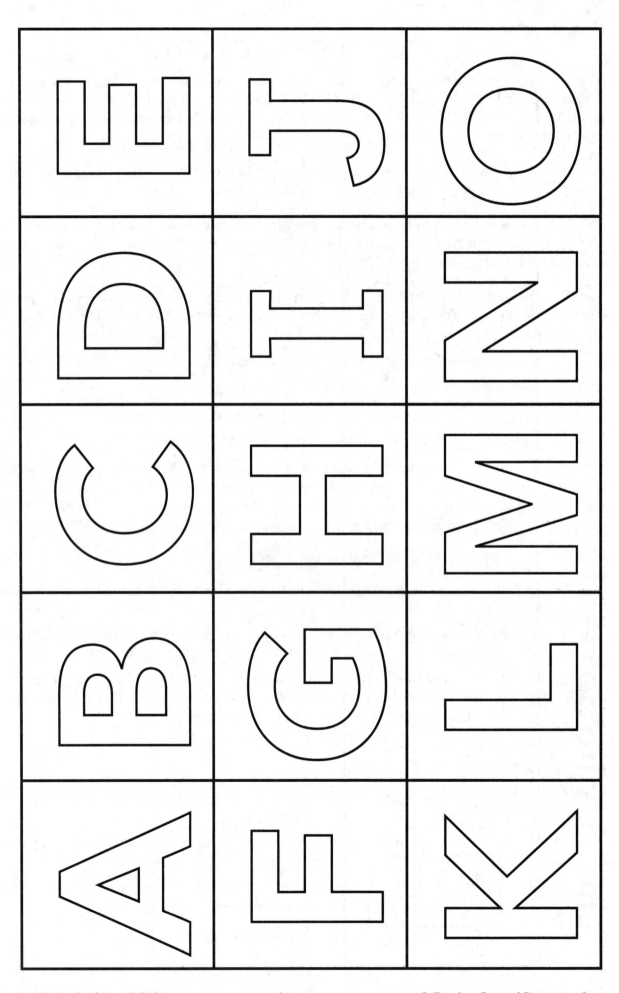

The Alphabet—Uppercase Flashcards (cont.)

T	S	R	Q	P
Y	X	W	V	U
		Z		

The Alphabet—Lowercase Flashcards

The Alphabet—Lowercase Flashcards (cont.)

t	s	r	q	p
y	x	w	v	u
		z		

Alphabet Stories
A and B

Read the story with your child. Circle the featured letter Aa in the story.

Apples and Aunt Annie Ant

Albert Ant and Angela Ant waited for Aunt Annie Ant to come to their anthill.

Aunt Annie Ant brought apples for Albert Ant and Angela Ant.

"Apples, apples, apples. Who wants an apple?" asked Aunt Annie Ant.

"We do. We do," said Albert Ant and Angela Ant.

Albert Ant and Angela Ant ate apples.

Aunt Annie Ant told Albert Ant and Angela Ant a story. After the story, Albert Ant and Angela Ant fell asleep.

Read the story with your child. Circle the featured letter Bb in the story.

Bobby and the Big Brown Bear

Bobby saw a big brown bear with a beautiful blue bag.

The big brown bear blew into the beautiful blue bag.

The beautiful blue bag got bigger and bigger.

The big brown bear pulled a big balloon out of the beautiful blue bag.

The brown bear gave the big balloon to Bobby.

Bobby said, "Thank you."

Then the big brown bear blew away with his beautiful blue bag.

Name _____

Letter Aa

Find the words that begin with the letter Aa. Circle the letter Aa and color the picture.

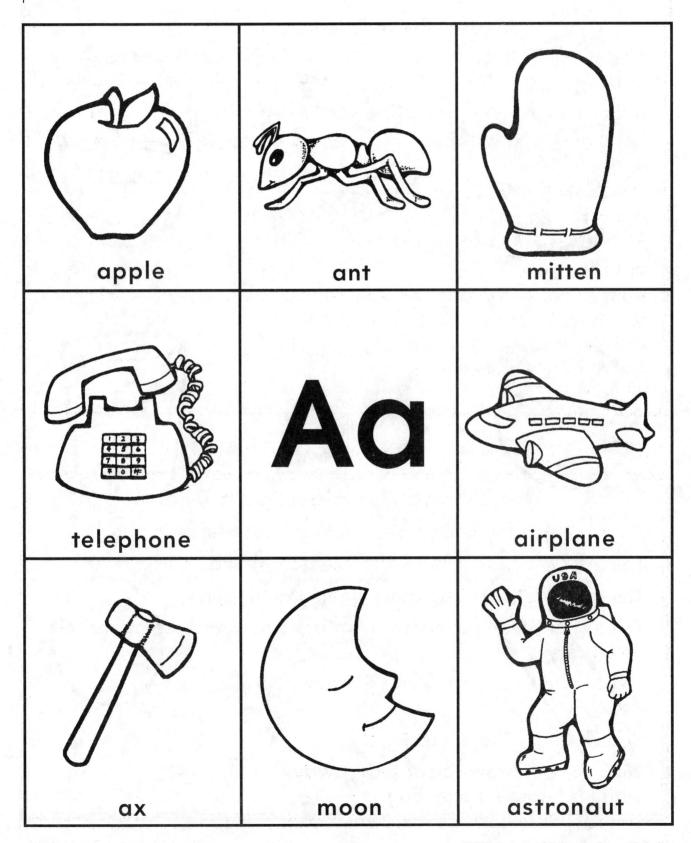

apple	ant	mitten
telephone	Aa	airplane
ax	moon	astronaut

Name _____

Letter Bb

Find the words that begin with the letter Bb. Circle the letter Bb and color the picture.

baby	flower	basket
ball	**Bb**	cup
pencil	bear	balloon

Alphabet Stories
C and D

Read the story with your child. Circle the featured letter Cc in the story.

Cat Food for Cami Cat

Cami Cat crept across the carpet. She was hungry.

Up the curtains she went.

Cami Cat tried to catch the cuckoo bird in the cuckoo clock.

Silly Cami Cat cannot eat a cuckoo bird! She eats cat food.

Cami Cat climbed down the curtains to her cat dish.

"Yum, yum. Cat food is good," said Cami Cat.

Cami Cat was tired after eating her cat food.

She curled up on the couch for a catnap.

Read the story with your child. Circle the featured letter Dd in the story.

Donald's Dogs and the Doughnuts

Donald's dogs were named Dusty and Dapper.

Dusty and Dapper liked to eat doughnuts with Donald.

Donald gave Dusty and Dapper dinner.

"What?" barked Dusty and Dapper. "This is just dog food."

Dusty and Dapper barked, "Doughnuts, doughnuts, doughnuts!"

Donald came running. "Do not bark, Dusty and Dapper. Eat your dog food."

Dusty and Dapper barked again. "Doughnuts, doughnuts, doughnuts!"

Donald came running again. "Do not bark, Dusty and Dapper. Here are some doughnuts!"

Then Dusty and Dapper were happy. They ate all the doughnuts.

Name_____

Letter Cc

Find the words that begin with the letter Cc. Circle the letter Cc and color the picture.

car

pear

cat

sun

Cc

cupcake

fish

castle

log

Name _____

Letter Dd

Find the words that begin with the letter Dd. Circle the letter Dd and color the picture.

dog	jacket	door
wagon	**Dd**	book
doughnut	deer	boat

Alphabet Stories
E and F

Read the story with your child. Circle the featured letter E e in the story.

The Enormous Ears

Everett Elephant had enormous ears.

Edgar Elephant had enormous ears.

"My ears are the most enormous," said Everett Elephant.

"My ears are the most enormous," said Edgar Elephant.

"I will decide," said Edward Elephant.

Edward Elephant measured Everett Elephant's ears.

Edward Elephant measured Edgar Elephant's ears.

"Everett Elephant and Edgar Elephant's ears are the same size," said Edward Elephant.

Everett Elephant and Edgar Elephant both have enormous ears.

Read the story with your child. Circle the featured letter F f in the story.

Flo Frog Fell

Frank Frog fixed four logs.

Flo Frog hopped onto the logs.

She fell into the water.

Frank Frog hopped into the water to help Flo Frog.

He helped Flo Frog out of the water.

Frank Frog helped Flo Frog sit on the four logs.

Frank Frog fed Flo Frog five flies.

Flo Frog was fine!

Name_____

Letter Ee

Find the words that begin with the letter Ee. Circle the letter Ee and color the picture.

elbow	elephant	chair
socks	**Ee**	elf
fox	egg	spoon

Name _____

Letter Ff

Find the words that begin with the letter Ff. Circle the letter Ff and color the picture.

feather	truck	fork
zebra	**Ff**	fish
frog	finger	box

Alphabet Stories
G and H

Read the story with your child. Circle the featured letter Gg in the story.

Grumpy Gus Goat

Gus Goat was grumpy. He was grumpy when Granny Goat said, "Good morning, Gus Goat." He was grumpy when Greta Goose said, "Good morning, Gus Goat." He was grumpy when Greta's goslings said, "Good morning, Gus Goat."

Granny Goat knew why Gus was grumpy.

"Gus Goat is hungry," said Granny Goat.

"Have some green grapes with us," said Greta Goose. "You will feel great."

Granny Goat, Greta Goose, Greta's goslings, and grumpy Gus Goat ate green grapes.

"Thank you, Greta Goose," said Granny Goat.

"Oh, thank you," said Gus Goat. "Now I feel great!"

Read the story with your child. Circle the featured letter Hh in the story.

Hanna Hen's Hay-filled Nest

Hanna Hen has her house on a hill. Hanna's hay-filled nest is in the house. Hanna Hen sits on her hay-filled nest. What is under Hanna Hen?

Under Hanna Hen are ten eggs. She sits on them to keep them hot.

"Peep, peep, peep."

Hanna Hen now has chicks in her hay-filled nest in her house on the hill.

Hooray for Hanna Hen! Hooray! Hooray!

Hooray for the ten chicks in Hanna Hen's hay-filled nest!

Name _____

Letter Gg

Find the words that begin with the letter Gg. Circle the letter Gg and color the picture.

goat

foot

girl

grapes

Gg

airplane

glass

monkey

gate

Name _____

Letter Hh

Find the words that begin with the letter Hh. Circle the letter Hh and color the picture.

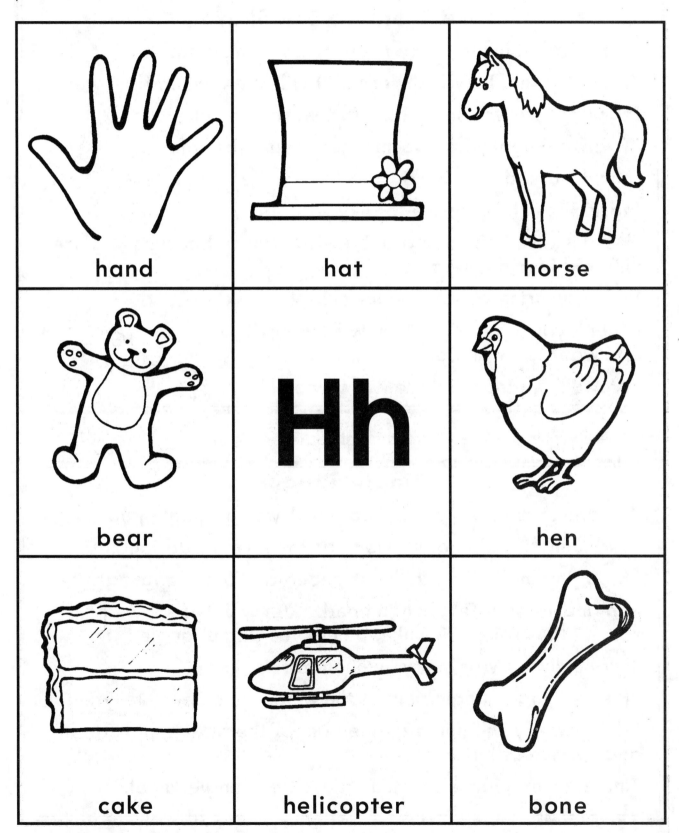

hand	hat	horse
bear	Hh	hen
cake	helicopter	bone

Alphabet Stories
I and J

Read the story with your child. Circle the featured letter Ii in the story.

We Want To Ice Skate

Ingrid Insect invited Inky Inchworm to ice skate.

"I am ill," said Inky Inchworm. "I will skate when I am well."

Ingrid Insect was sorry Inky Inchworm was ill.

"I will make Inky Inchworm a surprise," she said.

Ingrid worked very hard.

Ingrid took the surprise to Inky.

"Here is a surprise for you, Inky Inchworm, because you are ill," said Ingrid Insect.

Inky's surprise was a new ice skate!

"Thank you," said Inky. "Now I am not ill. I want to ice skate."

"Wow," said Ingrid. "We will go now!"

Read the story with your child. Circle the featured letter Jj in the story.

Jingle Jangle

Jan and Jessica Jellyfish liked jewelry to go jingle jangle.

Jerry Jellyfish did not like to hear the jewelry go jangle.

"Stop jingling!" Jerry Jellyfish shouted. "Stop jangling!"

Jan and Jessica Jellyfish jumped. "Jerry Jellyfish, we are sorry," they said. "We like to hear the jingle jangle."

Jerry Jellyfish was sorry he shouted.

"Please, jingle jangle part of the time," said Jerry Jellyfish.

"Our jewelry will jingle jangle part of the time," said Jan and Jessica Jellyfish.

Jingle, quiet, jangle, quiet. Jingle, quiet, jangle, quiet.

Name _____

Letter Ii

Find the words that begin with the letter Ii. Circle the letter Ii and color the picture.

ice cream	doll	ice cube
glasses	**Ii**	igloo
frog	island	flower

Name _____

Letter Jj

Find the words that begin with the letter Jj. Circle the letter Jj and color the picture.

guitar	butterfly	lamb
jellyfish	**Jj**	jar
glove	cake	leaf

Alphabet Stories
K and L

Read the story with your child. Circle the featured letter Kk in the story.

Ketchup for Kenny Kangaroo

Kenny Kangaroo was asleep in his mother's pocket.

Kenny Kangaroo kinked his tail and kicked his feet.

"I am hungry," said Kenny Kangaroo.

Mother Kangaroo hopped to the kitchen. She made ketchup in a kettle.

Kenny Kangaroo ate ketchup on his sandwich.

Kenny Kangaroo ate all the sandwich. "Excuse me, please," said Kenny Kangaroo.

Mother kissed Kenny Kangaroo and put him back into her pocket. Soon Kenny Kangaroo was asleep.

Read the story with your child. Circle the featured letter Ll in the story.

Lemon Lollipops

Little Lenny Lion licked a large lemon lollipop.

Little Lenny Lion laughed loudly.

Little Linda Lion looked around a log.

"May I lick a large lemon lollipop, too?" she asked loudly.

"I love licking large lemon lollipops," said little Linda Lion.

"Here is a large lemon lollipop for you, little Linda Lion," said little Lenny Lion.

The little lions licked and licked the large lemon lollipops.

Soon the large lemon lollipops were little lemon lollipops!

Letter Kk

Find the words that begin with the letter Kk. Circle the letter Kk and color the picture.

key

sun

doll

kangaroo

Kk

kite

king

ball

glasses

Letter Ll

Find the words that begin with the letter Ll. Circle the letter Ll and color the picture.

balloon	ladder	lion
lemon	**Ll**	pencil
leaf	cup	lamp

Alphabet Stories
M and N

Read the story with your child. Circle the featured letter Mm in the story.

Martin Mouse's Messy House

Martin Mouse had a mini house under a maple tree.

Mother Mouse was coming. What could Martin Mouse do?

Mud messed up the floor. Mail messed up the table.

Mittens messed up the chairs.

Martin Mouse worked very hard. When Mother Mouse came, the mess was gone!

Martin Mouse and Mother Mouse munched marshmallows and milk. They did not make a mess!

Read the story with your child. Circle the featured letter Nn in the story.

Nine Baby Nightingales

Mother Nightingale's nine baby nightingales napped nicely.

Night was coming. Nightingales wake up at night.

Mother Nightingale's nine baby nightingales napped.

They did not wake up.

"Wake up, baby nightingales. Wake up. Do not nap now!" said Mother Nightingale.

Still the nine baby nightingales napped.

"Help," said Mother Nightingale to Ned Nightingale. "Help me wake my nine napping nightingales."

Now it was night. Ned Nightingale sang a nightingale song, and the nine baby nightingales woke up.

"Thank you. Thank you, Ned Nightingale," said Mother Nightingale.

Name _____

Letter Mm

Find the words that begin with the letter Mm. Circle the letter Mm and color the picture.

moon

ladybug

mouse

cake

Mm

basket

monkey

beehive

mermaid

Name _____

Letter Nn

Find the words that begin with the letter Nn. Circle the letter Nn and color the picture.

nose

nail

nest

frog

Nn

needle

nine

ball

dinosaur

Alphabet Stories
O and P

Read the story with your child. Circle the featured letter Oo in the story.

Olives on Pizza

Ogden Octopus liked olives. Oliver Octopus did not like olives. Ogden Octopus and Oliver Octopus made a pizza.

"Stop," said Ogden Octopus. "Do not cook the pizza. I like olives."

"No," said Oliver Octopus. "I do not like olives."

"Olives," said Ogden Octopus.

"No olives," said Oliver Octopus.

"Yes, olives," said Ogden Octopus.

"No, no olives," said Oliver Octopus.

"I know what to do," said Ogden Octopus. "Make some pizza with olives. Make some pizza with no olives."

They were happy. Ogden Octopus ate pizza with olives. Oliver Octopus ate pizza without olives.

Read the story with your child. Circle the featured letter Pp in the story.

The Pigs Have A Picnic

Pablo and Polly Pig's parents planned a picnic.

"Prepare for the picnic. Please, pack pears and pizza." said Papa and Mama Pig.

Pablo and Polly Pig packed the picnic lunch.

Pitter-patter. Pitter-patter. Off went Pablo and Polly Pig for a picnic. Off went Papa and Mama Pig for a picnic.

Pablo and Polly Pig ate lots of pears and pizza. Papa and Mama Pig ate lots of pears and pizza.

What a perfect picnic day!

Name _____

Letter Oo

Find the words that begin with the letter Oo. Circle the letter Oo and color the picture.

octopus

box

owl

girl

Oo

goat

seal

orange

cake

Name _____

Letter Pp

Find the words that begin with the letter Pp. Circle the letter Pp and color the picture.

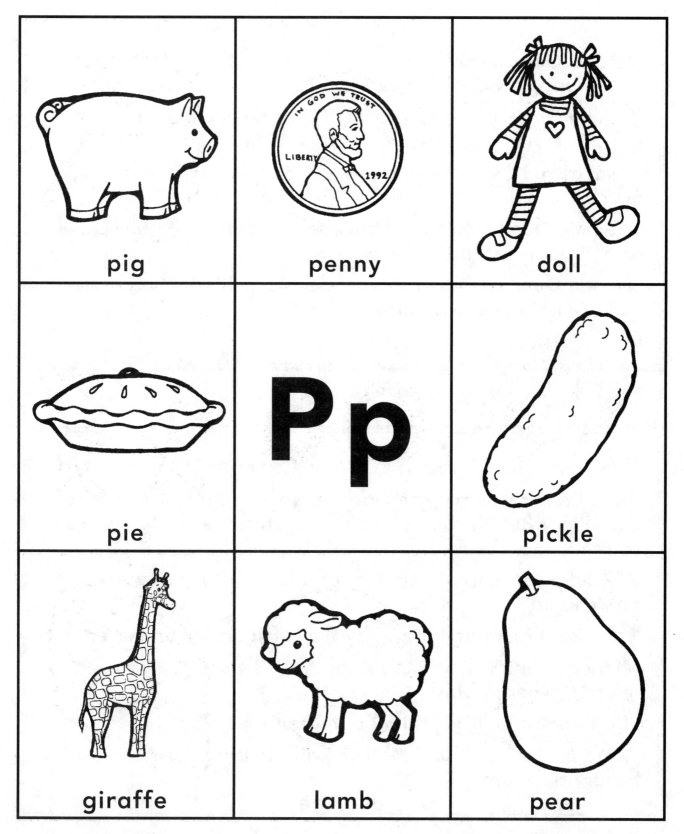

pig	penny	doll
pie	**Pp**	pickle
giraffe	lamb	pear

Alphabet Stories
Q and R

Read the story with your child. Circle the featured letter Q q in the story.

What Quacks?

Quentin Quail quickly ran home. Mother Quail said, "Quentin Quail, why do you run so fast?"

Quentin Quail hid under a quilt. "Why do you hide under a quilt, Quentin Quail?" asked Mother Quail.

"I am afraid," said Quentin Quail. "Something said quack, quack."

"Quentin Quail, you do not have to be afraid," Mother Quail said. "Ducks say quack, quack."

Quentin Quail came out from under the quilt. "Ducks quack, so I will not have to be afraid when I hear quack, quack" he said.

Read the story with your child. Circle the featured letter R r in the story.

"I Want a Raw Carrot!"

Ricky Rabbit was really hungry. He wanted a raw carrot to eat. Ricky Rabbit ran to the refrigerator. He saw a raw red radish.

"I want a raw carrot," said Ricky Rabbit. "I really want a raw carrot!"

Ricky Rabbit sat right down by the refrigerator and cried.

Mother Rabbit ran to Ricky Rabbit. "Why are you crying?" asked Mother Rabbit.

"I am really hungry," said Ricky Rabbit.

"Here is a carrot," said Mother Rabbit. Ricky Rabbit wasn't hungry anymore.

Name _____

Letter Qq

Find the words that begin with the letter Q q. Circle the letter Q q and color the picture.

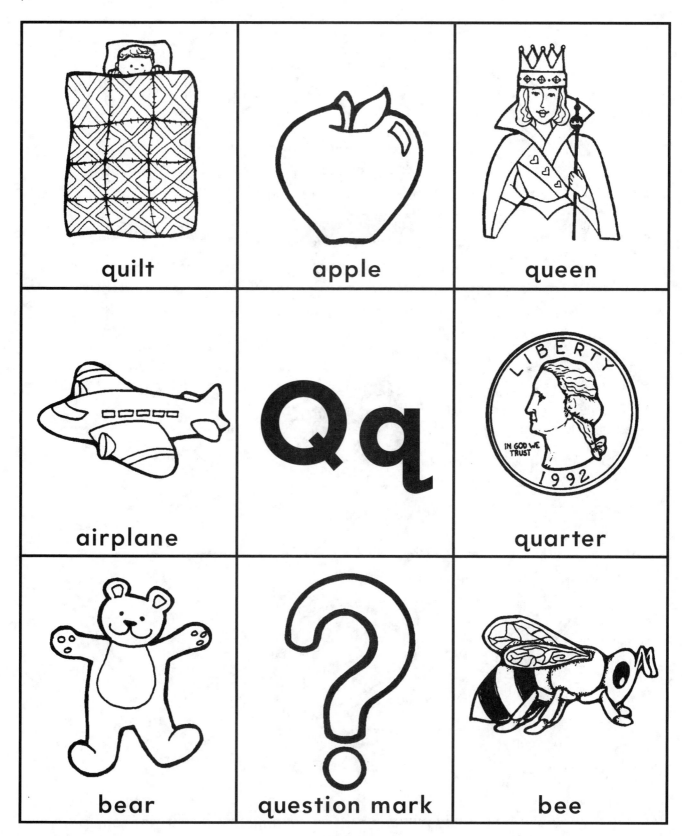

quilt	apple	queen
airplane	Qq	quarter
bear	question mark	bee

Name _____

Letter Rr

Find the words that begin with the letter Rr. Circle the letter Rr and color the picture.

pen	radio	refrigerator
bathtub	**Rr**	crab
rabbit	ball	rake

Alphabet Stories
S and T

Read the story with your child. Circle the featured letter Ss in the story.

Sally Sue, Sandy Sue, and the Skunk

Sally Sue and Sandy Sue were sisters walking to school.

Sally Sue stopped. "Smell, Sandy Sue!"

"Skunk," said Sandy Sue. "A smelly skunk! This skunk is too close!"

Sally Sue and Sandy Sue hid by a sand hill. A snail hid by the sand hill, too. The smelly skunk strolled by the sand hill.

"Skunks are super, super smelly!" said Sally Sue and Sandy Sue."

"The skunk is gone," said Sandy Sue. "We have to go to school."

"Good-bye, Snail," said the sisters as they strolled to school.

Read the story with your child. Circle the featured letter Tt in the story.

Ted Turtle and the Tall Boy

Ted Turtle liked to swim in the pond. He could swim fast.

One day a tall boy took Ted Turtle away from the pond.

The tall boy took Ted Turtle to a tent. Ted Turtle hid.

The tall boy went to sleep in the tent. Ted Turtle did not sleep.

Ted Turtle wanted to go home. Ted Turtle wanted to swim in the pond.

Ted Turtle walked slowly all night. He came to the pond. Ted Turtle swam away fast! He was glad he was home.

Name _____

Letter Ss

Find the words that begin with the letter Ss. Circle the letter Ss and color the picture.

scissors

skunk

cup

ball

Ss

sun

shirt

spoon

tree

Name_____

Letter Tt

Find the words that begin with the letter Tt. Circle the letter Tt and color the picture.

table

rose

turtle

monkey

Tt

truck

rocket

tooth

goat

Alphabet Stories
U and V

Read the story with your child. Circle the featured letter Uu in the story.

The Umbrellabird's Feather

"This is unusual," said Ulric Umbrellabird.

"My umbrellabird feather is not black. Usually my feathers are all black."

"This one is not black," said Ursula Umbrellabird.

Ulric Umbrellabird cried. He was upset.

"I will color it black," said Ursula Umbrellabird.

"What will I use?"

Ursula Umbrellabird used black crayon. The feather did not turn black. Ulric Umbrellabird cried some more.

Ursula Umbrellabird used black shoe polish. Now Ulric Umbrellabird's feather was black. Ulric Umbrellabird was happy.

Read the story with your child. Circle the featured letter Vv in the story.

Purple and Blue Violets

Veronica Viper liked purple violets. Vanessa Viper liked blue violets. Veronica Viper put purple violets in a vase. Vanessa Viper put blue violets in a vase.

"Mine are the prettiest violets," said Veronica Viper.

"Mine are the prettiest violets," said Vanessa Viper.

One long viper tail bumped the vases. One vase broke. Veronica Viper said, "I am sorry."

Vanessa Viper said, "I am sorry, too."

They put the purple and blue violets into one vase.

They were both happy.

Name _____

Letter Uu

Find the words that begin with the letter Uu. Circle the letter Uu and color the picture.

tea kettle	feather	umpire
frog	Uu	ant
umbrella	chair	umbrella bird

Letter Vv

Find the words that begin with the letter Vv. Circle the letter Vv and color the picture.

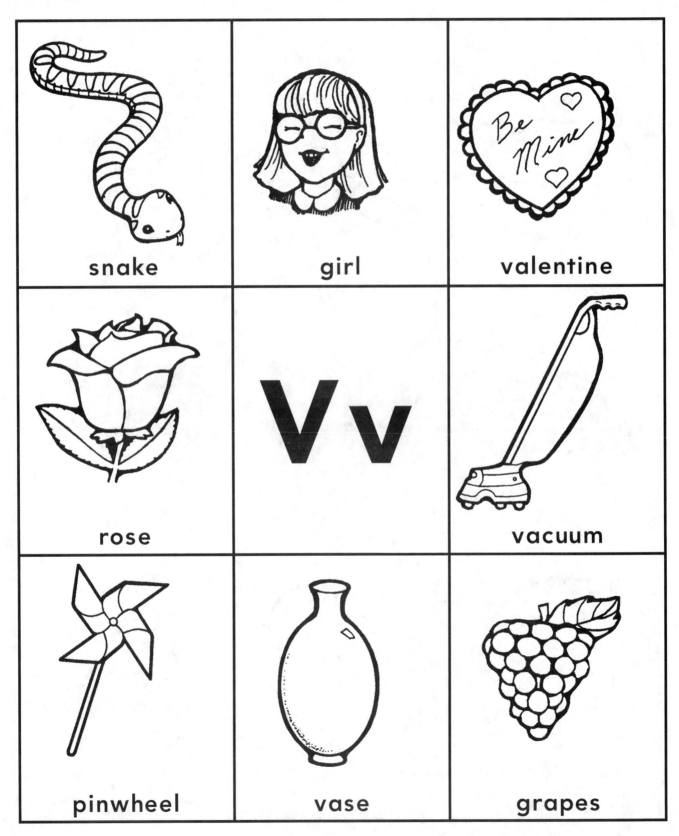

snake	girl	valentine
rose	**Vv**	vacuum
pinwheel	vase	grapes

40

Alphabet Stories
W and X

Read the story with your child. Circle the featured letter Ww in the story.

Woodrow Walrus Wants Watermelon

Woodrow Walrus waded in the water.

"That's weird," said Woodrow Walrus. "I want watermelon."

"Watermelon is not in the water. Walruses do not eat watermelon.

"Walruses eat fish!"

Woodrow Walrus looked at Winnie Walrus. "That's weird," he said. "Now I want fish."

Woodrow Walrus waded in the water to get some.

Read the story with your child. Circle the featured letter Xx in the story.

A Box for Dixie Fox

"Alex," said Dixie Fox, "please, find me a box."

"How can I find a box?" asked Alex Fox. "I do not know where to find a box."

"Mr. Ox may have a box at his store," said Dixie Fox.

Alex Fox and Dixie Fox went to see Mr. Ox.

"Mr. Ox," said Alex Fox.

"Do you have a box?"

Mr. Ox had six boxes at his store!

Dixie Fox took a box. She was a happy fox.

Name _____

Letter Ww

Find the words that begin with the letter Ww. Circle the letter Ww and color the picture.

star	walrus	pie
wagon	**Ww**	watermelon
wood	dog	window

Letter Xx

Find the words that have the letter Xx in them. Circle the letter Xx and color the picture.

fox	book	kite
ax	Xx	box
elephant	six	apple

Alphabet Stories
Y and Z

Read the story with your child. Circle the featured letter Yy in the story.

Yetta Yak's Yellow Bowl

Yetta Yak was hungry. Yetta Yak liked yogurt in her yellow bowl.

"Where is my yellow bowl?" asked Yetta Yak.

Yetta Yak looked in her yellow cupboard.

There was no yellow bowl in the yellow cupboard or in her yellow sink.

"Yuk," she said. "My yellow bowl is dirty."

Yetta Yak washed her yellow bowl in her yellow sink.

Yetta Yak put yogurt in her yellow bowl. "Yum, yum, this is good yogurt in my yellow bowl."

Yetta Yak ate all the yogurt. She put her dirty yellow bowl in her yellow sink. She liked her yogurt.

Read the story with your child. Circle the featured letter Zz in the story.

Zoomy Zed Zebra

Zed Zebra zoomed past Zeke the zookeeper into the barn.

"Zikes!" said Mother Zebra. "Zed Zebra, why do you zip and zoom around so fast?"

Zip, zing! Zed Zebra zoomed out of the zoo barn past Zeke the zookeeper. Zip, zing! Little Zed Zebra zoomed into the zoo barn again.

"Zed Zebra, stop!" said Mother Zebra. "Zed Zebra, you zoom too fast. You need a nap"

Z-Z-Z-Z-Z-Z. Zip. Zed Zebra was fast asleep!

Name _____

Letter Yy

Find the words that have the letter Yy in them. Circle the letter Yy and color the picture.

yarn	**chair**	**door**
yoyo	**Yy**	**yolk**
moon	**yak**	**spoon**

Name _____

Letter Zz

Find the words that have the letter Zz in them. Circle the letter Zz and color the picture.

key	zipper	dinosaur
zebra	Zz	doll
jacket	zero	zigzag

Do You Know Your Alphabet?

Read the letters in the alphabet. Put your finger under each letter and say its name.

A	B	C	D	E
F	G	H	I	J
K	L	M	N	O
P	Q	R	S	T
U	V	W	X	Y
		Z		

Which Letters Are Missing?

Fill in the blanks with the missing letters of the alphabet. Write both the uppercase and lowercase letter.

___ ___ **Bb** ___ ___ ___ ___ **Ee**

___ ___ **Gg** **Hh** ___ ___ **Jj** **Kk**

Ll ___ ___ ___ ___ ___ ___ **Pp**

Qq **Rr** ___ ___ **Tt** **Uu**

___ ___ **Ww** ___ ___ ___ ___ **Zz**